MW01221772

Scotland
Travel Guide

The Ultimate Travel Guide to Exploring the Best Part Of Scotland

Edward Noah

All rights reserved. No part of this publication may be reproduced, distributed, or transmitted in any form or by any means, including photocopying, recording, or other electronic or mechanical methods, without the prior written permission of the publisher, except in the case of brief quotations embodied in critical reviews and certain other noncommercial uses permitted by copyright law.

Copyright © Edward Noah

Table of Contents

Short History

Scotland is a country in the northern section of the British Isles, with a rich history extending back thousands of years. The land was formerly populated by several indigenous groups, including the Picts and the Celts before it was eventually established by the Scots, who gave the country its name.

The earliest known human settlements in Scotland date back to the Mesolithic period, circa 8000 BC. These early people lived by hunting and fishing, and evidence of their societies may be discovered in the shape of stone circles and burial sites.

During the Bronze Age, from roughly 2000 BC to 800 BC, the Beaker civilization emerged in Scotland. This was a time of technological growth when mankind learned to produce bronze tools and weapons.

In the Iron Age, which spanned from 800 BC until the Roman conquest in AD 43, the Picts emerged as a dominant force in Scotland. They were noted for their striking tattoos and were skilled warriors. The Romans sought to subjugate the Picts but were never able to entirely subdue them.

In the early medieval period, Scotland was divided into various kingdoms, notably the Pictish kingdom of Fortriu, the Dal Riata kingdom of the Gaels, and the Brittonic kingdom of Strathclyde. In the 9th century, Kenneth MacAlpin, the king of Dal Riata, became the first ruler to unite Scotland under a single monarchy.

Throughout the Middle Ages, Scotland had an era of cultural and intellectual growth known as the Scottish Renaissance. This period saw the development of luminaries such as the philosopher John Duns Scotus, the poet Robert Burns, and the historian George Buchanan.

In the 16th century, Scotland was severely affected by the Protestant Reformation, which led to the founding of the Presbyterian Church. This period also saw a fight for power between the Scottish monarchs and the English monarchy, as well as conflicts between rival groups inside Scotland.

Throughout the 17th century, Scotland saw considerable political and social upheaval, including the Wars of the Three Kingdoms and the Glorious Revolution. In 1707, the Act of Union was passed, which unified Scotland and England into a single political entity known as Great Britain.

During the 18th and 19th centuries, Scotland witnessed a period of tremendous industrialization and urbanization, as well as great cultural and intellectual breakthroughs. The Scottish Enlightenment saw the development of figures such as Adam Smith, David Hume, and James Watt, who made substantial contributions to subjects like economics, philosophy, and engineering.

Throughout the 20th century, Scotland played a prominent role in both World War I and World War II and saw substantial social and economic changes in the post-war period. In the late 20th and early 21st centuries, there has been a resurgent interest in Scottish identity and independence, with the founding of the Scottish Parliament in 1999 and a referendum on independence in 2014.

Today, Scotland is a lively and diverse country with a rich cultural legacy and a strong sense of national identity. Its history has been formed by a number of elements, from its topography and natural resources to its political and social changes, and continues to be shaped by the problems and opportunities of the current day.

Geography

Scotland is divided into three primary regions: the Highlands, the Central Lowlands, and the Southern Uplands. Each region has its unique features that make Scotland an outstanding destination to visit.

The Highlands, occupying the northwestern section of Scotland, is defined by its steep topography, wide coastline, and numerous islands. The highest peak in Scotland, Ben Nevis, is located in the Highlands, rising to a height of 1,345 meters. The region is also home to many famous lochs (lakes) such as Loch Ness, Loch Lomond, and Loch Maree. The Highlands are sparsely populated, with many regions remaining uninhabited, making it a wonderful location for nature lovers and outdoor enthusiasts.

The Central Lowlands, located between the Highlands and the Southern Uplands, is the most populous and economically important region of Scotland. This area is noted by its gently undulating hills, large valleys, and fertile farms. The region is home to Scotland's two main cities, Edinburgh and Glasgow, as well as other prominent towns and cities such as Stirling, Falkirk, and Perth. The River Clyde and the Forth and Clyde Canal, which links the east and west coastlines of Scotland, are two of the main rivers in this region.

The Southern Uplands, located in the south of Scotland, is a range of hills and valleys that span from the border with England to the Firth of Clyde. The region is noted by its lush green valleys, open moorland, and upland grassland. The Southern Uplands are home to Scotland's highest village, Wanlockhead, and the highest village in the UK, Leadhills.

The region is sparsely populated, with small towns and villages dispersed over the landscape.

Scotland's coastline is approximately 6,160 km long and is home to over 790 islands, including the Orkney Islands, the Shetland Islands, and the Hebrides. The islands are a key tourist destination, with their gorgeous landscapes, jagged coasts, and plentiful wildlife. The shoreline is also home to numerous lovely fishing villages, such as Saint Andrews, Anstruther, and Pittenweem.

Scotland's climate is oceanic, with warm winters and cool summers. The country's location has a major effect on shaping its climate. The Atlantic Ocean and the North Sea soften Scotland's climate, resulting in pleasant temperatures throughout the year. Nonetheless, the Highlands have more harsh weather conditions, with considerable snowfall in winter and lower temperatures throughout the year.

Scotland is also home to various national parks, including Cairngorms National Park, Lake Lomond and The Trossachs National Park, and the Island of Skye. These parks provide visitors an opportunity to experience Scotland's diverse landscapes and plentiful wildlife up close. The Cairngorms National Park is the largest national park in the UK and is home to some of Scotland's most stunning landscapes, including the Cairngorm Mountains and Lake Morlich.

The Isle of Skye, located off the west coast of Scotland, is famed for its rocky shoreline, stunning mountain ranges, and attractive settlements.

Visitors Must Know Things Before Visiting

There are several things that travelers must know before visiting Scotland to make the most out of their trip. In this area, we will explain the tourist must-know topics before visiting Scotland.

Currency
Scotland uses Pound Sterling as its means of exchange. It is recommended that travelers exchange their cash before arriving in Scotland to avoid the trouble of exchanging money while in the country. Credit and debit cards are frequently accepted in Scotland, however, it is always a good idea to keep some cash on hand for smaller transactions.

Weather
The weather in Scotland can be unpredictable, therefore it is vital to pack for all kinds of weather conditions. Scotland has a marine climate, which means it can be cold, damp, and windy at times. Summers are generally warm, and winters are frequently frigid, with occasional snowfall. It is usually a good idea to pack a waterproof jacket, warm clothing, and suitable walking shoes.

Language
The official language of Scotland is English, but Scottish Gaelic is also spoken in several regions of the country. While most Scots speak English, the accent can be tough for outsiders to comprehend, therefore it is crucial to be patient when interacting with locals.

Accommodation

Scotland provides a wide selection of housing alternatives, from inexpensive hostels to luxury hotels. Visitors can also choose to stay in traditional Scottish B&Bs or self-catering cottages. It is generally a good idea to reserve accommodation in advance, especially during the busy tourist season.

Transportation

Scotland has a well-developed transportation infrastructure, and travelers can choose between buses, trains, and taxis to get about. Hiring a car is also an option, but tourists must be warned that driving in Scotland can be tough, especially on narrow roads.

Culture and History

Scotland has a rich cultural and historical past, and tourists can discover this through the country's numerous museums, art galleries, and historical monuments. The Scottish National Museum, the National Galleries of Scotland, and Edinburgh Castle are just a few of the must-visit places for travelers interested in Scotland's culture and history.

Etiquette

Travelers must be aware of Scottish etiquette, which involves honoring the country's culture, traditions, and values. It is crucial to dress correctly when visiting holy places and to be respectful of local customs and traditions. Tipping is widely expected in Scotland, with a customary amount of 10-15% in restaurants and bars.

Top Scotland Websites

Going to a new place can be intimidating, especially if you are not familiar with the area. Fortunately, there are various touring websites accessible that can help you travel and see Scotland. In this part, we will cover the finest touring websites for Scotland.

VisitScotland

VisitScotland is the official tourist board for Scotland. The website gives detailed information about Scotland's top attractions, events, and accommodation options. It also provides guides to help you plan your trip. You can search for individual attractions or explore them through numerous categories such as castles, museums, and nature reserves. The website also offers discounts and special offers on a range of activities and experiences.
Website: www.visitscotland.com

Google Maps

Google Maps is a vital tool for travelers. It gives directions, real-time traffic updates, and information on surrounding attractions and eateries. It also allows users to save maps offline, making it easier to navigate in locations with poor connectivity.

TripAdvisor

TripAdvisor is one of the most popular travel apps and websites in the world. It gives information about hotels, airlines, restaurants, and attractions in numerous destinations across the world. Customers may read reviews, browse images, and book their bookings straight through the app or website.

Website: www.tripadvisor.com

Viator
Viator is a website that offers tours and activities in various destinations across the world. Customers can choose from a number of alternatives, including sightseeing trips, cooking lessons, and outdoor adventures.
Website: www.viator.com

Skyscanner
Skyscanner is a travel search engine that analyzes rates across numerous flights, hotels, and car rental companies. It allows customers to get the greatest bargains on flights and accommodations, saving them time and money.
Website: www.skyscanner.net

Kayak
Kayak is another travel search engine that compares prices across various airlines, hotels, and car rental companies. It also features a function called "Explore" that allows users to search for destinations based on their budget.
Website: www.kayak.com

Edinburgh Bus Tours
Edinburgh Bus Tours is a website that gives a hop-on-hop-off bus tour around Edinburgh. The tour takes you to all of the city's greatest sights, including Edinburgh Castle, the Royal Mile, and the Scottish Parliament. The website contains live audio commentary that provides information about each site as you pass by.
Website: www.edinburghtour.com

Top Activities

Scotland boasts a wide choice of physical outdoor activities, including hiking, cycling, kayaking, fishing, and golfing. In this section, we will explore each of these actions and provide a detailed description of what they include.

Hiking

One of the most popular hiking places in Scotland is the Scottish Highlands. This region is noted for its majestic mountain ranges, including the famed Ben Nevis, the highest peak in the United Kingdom. The Highlands provide a variety of hiking trails ranging from casual strolls to demanding multi-day hikes. Among the most popular routes in the Scottish Highlands include the West Highland Way, the Great Glen Way, and the Speyside Way.

The West Highland Way is a 154-kilometer trail that starts in Milngavie and concludes in Fort William, passing through the spectacular vistas of Loch Lomond, Rannoch Moor, and Glen Coe along the way. The trail can take anything from 5 to 9 days to finish, depending on your pace and how much time you want to spend enjoying the landscape. The Great Glen Way is another popular trail in the Scottish Highlands, spanning approximately 117 kilometers from Fort William to Inverness, going through the Great Glen and along the banks of Lake Ness.

For those seeking a shorter hike, there are lots of possibilities in the Scottish Lowlands. The Borders Abbeys Way is a 109-kilometer trail that leads walkers through the scenic Scottish Borders region, passing through several medieval abbeys along the way. The Fife Coastal Walk is another popular track, spanning about 117 kilometers along the gorgeous Fife coastline, affording stunning views of the North Sea and the surrounding landscape.

Hiking in Scotland is not just about the gorgeous landscapes, it's also about the culture and history of the place. Scotland is home to a rich history and culture, and hikers may learn about the country's past while exploring its rough landscape. The West Highland Way, for example, goes through several historic towns and villages, including Drymen, Tyndrum, and Kinlochleven, affording a look into the country's past. The trail also passes past various ancient landmarks, including the remnants of Kilchurn Castle and the remains of St. Conan's Kirk.

When trekking in Scotland, it's crucial to be prepared for the weather. Scotland is known for its variable weather, and hikers should be prepared for rain, wind, and even snow, regardless of the time of year. It's crucial to wear appropriate clothing and footwear and to carry a waterproof jacket and extra layers to remain warm. Hikers should also bring plenty of food and drink, as well as a map and compass, to ensure they stay on course.

Cycling

Cycling in Scotland is a popular hobby for visitors and locals alike. With its gorgeous scenery, rolling hills, and scenic routes, Scotland is a great destination for cycling aficionados. Whether you are an experienced biker or a beginner, there is a path for everyone to appreciate.

The Scottish geographical diversity gives a choice of riding experiences, from tough mountain climbs to pleasant beach rides. One of the most popular cycling routes in Scotland is the North Coast 500, a 500-mile round route that takes riders through some of the most spectacular landscapes in Scotland. The route takes in the rugged beauty of the Scottish Highlands, the spectacular coasts of the North Sea and the Atlantic Ocean, and the breathtaking magnificence of the Scottish Islands.

Another popular cycling route in Scotland is the Lochs and Glens route, which takes riders through the spectacular landscapes of Loch Lomond, the Trossachs National Park, and the Cairngorms National Park. This route is great for people searching for a more peaceful cycling experience, with mild rolling hills and stunning views.

For those searching for a more strenuous cycling experience, Scotland features some of the most challenging mountains climbs in the Country. The Bealach na Bà, located in the Scottish Highlands, is one of the most demanding mountains passes in Scotland, with steep grades and hairpin curves. The ascent rewards cyclists with excellent vistas of the surrounding terrain, making it a must-ride for experienced cyclists.

One of the attractions of cycling in Scotland is the number of lodging alternatives available. Cyclists can choose to a tent, stay in hostels or bed & breakfasts, or select more luxurious lodging in hotels or lodges. Numerous hotel companies in Scotland cater specifically to bikers, offering facilities for bike storage and maintenance, as well as recommendations for local routes and riding guides.

Several of the cycling routes in Scotland take in historic attractions, such as castles and old ruins, as well as cultural landmarks, such as art galleries and museums. The city of Edinburgh, the capital of Scotland, is a popular destination for bikers, having a choice of historic and cultural sites to explore.

While planning a bicycle trip to Scotland, it is crucial to be prepared for the weather. Scotland is noted for its varied weather, with rain and wind a typical occurrence. Cyclists should pack proper clothing and equipment for all weather conditions, including waterproof jackets and pants, thermal layers, and sturdy cycling shoes.

Cycling in Scotland is a terrific opportunity to enjoy the beauty and diversity of this stunning country. With a multitude of routes and experiences accessible, from demanding mountain climbs to peaceful beach rides, there is something for everyone to enjoy.

Water Sports

Apart from its stunning scenery, Scotland also provides a wide selection of adventurous water activities that attract tourists from all over the world. The country is surrounded by water on three sides, giving a plethora of water sports activities for adventure seekers.

One of the most popular water sports in Scotland is surfing. The west coast of Scotland is particularly famed for its surfing areas. The coastline is lined with several surf locations that cater to surfers of all levels, from beginners to pros. One of the most popular surfing sites in Scotland is Thurso East, which is noted for its powerful and regular waves. Other popular surfing areas include Tiree, Machrihanish, and Pease Bay.

Another water sport that is gaining popularity in Scotland is stand-up paddleboarding (SUP). SUP involves standing on a board and using a paddle to move oneself through the water. Scotland's quiet lochs and sheltered bays give great conditions for SUP. It is a terrific way to explore the country's natural beauty and fauna up close. Some of the top SUP sites in Scotland are Loch Lomond, Loch Morlich, and Loch Tay.

Kayaking is another prominent water sport in Scotland. The country's various lochs, rivers, and sea lochs give kayakers a broad range of paddling options. Kayakers may explore Scotland's rocky beaches, quiet lochs, and fast-flowing rivers. The River Spey is particularly popular among kayakers due to its fast-flowing rapids and magnificent surroundings.

Scotland's pristine seas also make it an attractive destination for snorkeling and diving. The country's shores are home to a rich assortment of marine life, including seals, dolphins, and sharks. The Firth of Forth is a particularly popular snorkeling destination due to its clean waters and richness of marine life. Diving enthusiasts can explore the wrecks and underwater landscapes off the coast of the Isle of Skye and the Orkney Islands.

For those searching for an adrenaline boost, white water rafting is a must-try water sport in Scotland. The country's fast-flowing rivers, like the River Tay and River Spey, give excellent rafting possibilities for thrill-seekers. The rapids range from grade 1 to grade 5, catering to rafters of all skill levels.

Fly fishing is another prominent water-based hobby in Scotland. The country is famous for its salmon and trout fishing, which attracts anglers from all over the world. Scotland's rivers and lochs provide excellent fishing opportunities for both novices and expert anglers. The River Tweed is one of the most popular fly fishing destinations in Scotland.

Skiing and Snowboarding

Skiing and snowboarding in Scotland may not be the first thing that springs to mind when planning a winter sports holiday, but Scotland offers a unique and fascinating experience for travelers. With a range of ski resorts and winter sports activities accessible, Scotland is a perfect location for both novices and expert skiers and snowboarders.

Scotland has five significant ski resorts, with the largest being the Cairngorm Ski Resort. Situated in the heart of the Cairngorms National Park, the resort provides a variety of skiing and snowboarding lines, from beginner slopes to tough black runs. The resort also includes the UK's tallest funicular railway, which takes guests up to the summit of the mountain in just eight minutes, affording amazing views of the surrounding terrain.

The Glenshee Ski Centre is another major ski resort in Scotland, featuring the largest skiing area in the country. With 22 lifts and 36 lines, the resort has something for everyone, including a specialized beginners' section and numerous tough routes for advanced skiers and snowboarders. Glenshee also offers night skiing, allowing tourists to enjoy the slopes after dark.

The Nevis Range Ski Centre, located near Fort William, is another popular location for winter sports aficionados. With a selection of runs catering to all abilities, the resort also offers beautiful vistas of Ben Nevis. The resort also includes the UK's only mountain gondola, transporting visitors up to 650m above sea level and affording panoramic views of the surrounding landscape.

Other ski resorts in Scotland include the Lecht Ski Centre, which offers a selection of slopes for all abilities, as well as a snow park and a tubing park for non-skiers, and the Glencoe Mountain Resort, which offers skiing and snowboarding on Scotland's oldest ski area.

In addition to these ski resorts, Scotland provides a number of other winter sports activities, such as cross-country skiing, snowshoeing, and sledding. The Cairngorm Mountain Resort, for example, offers cross-country skiing tracks that wind through the stunning Caledonian pine forests, while the Nevis Range Ski Centre offers snowshoeing tours that allow guests to enjoy the winter terrain on foot.

While arranging a skiing or snowboarding trip to Scotland, it is necessary to be informed of the weather conditions. Scotland's ski season normally runs from December to April, however, snowfall can be erratic, and some years may see less snow than others. It is also necessary to be prepared for cold and damp conditions, with adequate clothing and equipment.

Climbing

Scotland is a mecca for adventure lovers, and one of the most thrilling experiences that travelers may have is climbing its peaks. Scotland offers a number of alternatives for climbers, from moderate walks to difficult mountain treks. The country is recognized for its rough landscapes, towering cliffs, and breathtaking mountain ranges, which attract climbers from all over the world.

Climbing in Scotland is a popular pastime throughout the year, although the best time to climb is generally from April to October. The weather conditions in Scotland can be demanding, and climbers need to be prepared for rapid changes in weather. It is also vital to examine the weather forecast and local circumstances before commencing any climb.

Scotland features a range of climbing routes, including rock climbing, winter climbing, and mountaineering. Rock climbing is a popular hobby in Scotland, and there are numerous routes to choose from. The most popular climbing sites are in the northwest, including the Torridon and Assynt districts, as well as the Isle of Skye. These places offer some of the most beautiful scenery in Scotland, with towering cliffs and rocky peaks.

Winter climbing is a more strenuous exercise that demands training and technique. Scotland is famed for its winter climbing, which takes place from December to March. The Scottish Highlands offer some of the best winter climbing possibilities in Europe, with demanding routes on snow and ice. Some of the most popular winter climbing areas include Ben Nevis, Glencoe, and the Cairngorms.

Mountaineering is another popular pastime in Scotland, which requires ascending peaks exceeding 3,000 feet. The Scottish highlands, or Munros, offer some of the best mountaineering options in the UK. There are 282 Munros in Scotland, with the tallest being Ben Nevis, which reaches 1,345 meters. Climbing a Munro is a rewarding experience, and many climbers strive to climb all of them.

There are several climbing guides and instructors in Scotland that can provide guidance and help to climbers of all abilities. Climbing lessons are provided for beginners, while more experienced climbers can hire a guide to take them on more tough routes. It is crucial to hire a recognized guide or instructor and to confirm that they have the relevant qualifications and expertise.

Climbing in Scotland can be a dangerous hobby, and climbers need to be mindful of the risks involved. The weather conditions in Scotland can vary suddenly, and climbers need to be prepared for sudden storms, strong winds, and snowfall. It is crucial to bring the relevant equipment, including a map, compass, and appropriate clothes, and to ensure that you are familiar with the terrain before commencing a climb.

Scotland offers a distinct cultural experience for travelers. The country has a rich history and culture, with many traditional Scottish activities and festivals taking place throughout the year. Guests can enjoy Scottish friendliness and sample traditional Scottish cuisine, including haggis, neeps, and tatties.

Climbing in Scotland is a thrilling and satisfying pastime that offers a unique experience for tourists. Scotland's mountainous landscapes and steep peaks attract climbers from all over the world, and there are routes accessible for climbers of all levels. Nonetheless, it is crucial to be aware of the risks involved with climbing and to take the appropriate steps to protect your safety.

Fishing

Among the many sports, fishing is one of the most popular and sought-after pastimes by tourists who visit Scotland. Scotland boasts over 30,000 freshwater lochs (lakes) and over 6,000 miles of coastline which makes it a fantastic destination for fishing aficionados. This section will provide a thorough description of fishing in Scotland, including what types of fish can be caught, when to fish, and where to fish.

Scotland is home to a broad array of fish species that can be caught in both freshwater and saltwater regions. In freshwater, fishermen can locate species such as salmon, trout, pike, and grayling. Salmon is one of the most popular fish species to catch in Scotland and is sometimes referred to as the 'King of Fish'. Scottish salmon is well-known for its flavor and quality, and it can weigh up to 30 pounds. Trout is another common freshwater fish that can be caught in

Scotland. Brown trout and rainbow trout are the most common species found in Scottish lochs.

In saltwater, fishermen can target species such as cod, haddock, plaice, pollock, and mackerel. Cod and haddock are the most popular species for anglers to capture and are found in abundance around the Scottish coastline.

The fishing season in Scotland is normally from March to October, with the peak season being from June to September. During the peak season, the weather is warmer, and the water is at its best temperature for fishing. Nonetheless, fishing is feasible all year round, with some species being particularly active during the winter months.

In freshwater, trout fishing is best from April to October, with peak season being from May to August. Salmon fishing is excellent from June to October, with peak season being from July to September. In saltwater, cod and haddock can be taken all year round, with the peak season being from October to March.

There are several spots in Scotland where anglers can fish for both freshwater and saltwater species. Some of the most popular freshwater destinations include Loch Lomond, Loch Ness, River Tay, and River Spey. These spots provide spectacular views of the Scottish environment and an opportunity to catch some of the most sought-after fish species in Scotland.

The Scottish coastline offers some of the top fishing areas in Europe. Some of the most popular sites include Aberdeen, Ullapool, Oban, and the Island of Skye. These areas provide fishermen the opportunity to catch species such as cod, haddock, plaice, and pollock, as well as the chance to see some of Scotland's spectacular wildlife, such as seals, dolphins, and whales.

For travelers who are new to fishing or who wish to experience the greatest fishing areas in Scotland, guided fishing trips are an ideal alternative. Guided fishing trips give anglers with expert guides who know the best spots to fish, as well as suggestions and strategies for catching fish. Guided fishing trips also include all the essential equipment, including rods, reels, and bait.

Scotland has a vast variety of fish species to target, both in freshwater and saltwater sites and the fishing season lasts from March to October. With so many beautiful spots to fish, guided fishing tours are an excellent alternative for travelers who want to make the most of their fishing experience in Scotland.

Wildlife Watching

One of the most iconic wildlife species that may be spotted in Scotland is the red deer. These gorgeous creatures can be found in many regions of Scotland, including the Cairngorms National Park and the Isle of Mull. The greatest time to watch red deer is during the autumn rutting season when stags compete for mates and put on a display of roaring and posturing.

Another distinctive animal that can be observed in Scotland is the red squirrel. These lovely critters are distributed throughout the country, although are most usually sighted in forest regions. Visitors can witness them scurrying around tree branches, picking nuts and seeds, or simply sunbathing in the sun. Although formerly threatened with extinction, conservation efforts have managed to conserve the red squirrel population in Scotland.

For bird watchers, Scotland is a delight. The country is home to approximately 500 kinds of birds, including sea eagles, puffins, and ospreys. The island of Mull, off the west coast of Scotland, is one of the greatest spots to watch sea eagles, while the Isle of Skye is a prime location for observing puffins during the mating season. Ospreys can be spotted at a number of locations throughout Scotland, including Loch Garten in the Cairngorms National Park.

Scotland is also home to a variety of marine creatures, including whales, dolphins, and seals. Tourists can take boat rides from a number of spots around the coast to see these wonderful creatures up close. The Moray Firth on the east coast of Scotland is one of the greatest areas to watch dolphins, while the west coast is a prime location for spotting minke whales and basking sharks. Seals can be observed in several spots around the coast, including the Island of Skye and the Firth of Forth.

Visitors to Scotland can also witness the stunning sight of hundreds of seabirds breeding on the cliffs of the country's rough shoreline. The Island of May, off the coast of Fife, is home to one of the largest colonies of puffins in the world, as well as a variety of other seabirds such as guillemots, razorbills, and kittiwakes.

Scotland is a sanctuary for wildlife lovers, offering a vast selection of wildlife species and areas to explore. From the majestic red deer to the charming red squirrel, Scotland presents a unique opportunity to observe the beauties of nature up close. Whether you're a bird watcher, a marine animal fanatic, or simply a lover of nature, Scotland is the perfect destination for your next excursion.

Golfing

Scotland is a world-renowned destination for golfers, boasting some of the most challenging and spectacular courses in the world. The country is renowned as the "home of golf" because the current game developed in Scotland in the 15th century. Nowadays, golf is still firmly rooted in Scottish society, with over 550 courses across the country.

One of the biggest draws for golfers visiting Scotland is the country's links courses. Links courses are coastal courses with natural terrain that includes sand dunes, thick grasses, and undulating fairways. These courses provide a unique challenge for golfers, with unpredictable wind patterns and challenging shots over and around obstacles. Some of the most notable links courses in Scotland include Saint Andrews Old Course, Royal Troon, and Turnberry.

One of the most crucial things to take in mind when arranging a golf trip to Scotland is the weather. Scotland's environment may be unpredictable, with rain and wind being regular factors on the course. But, this shouldn't prevent golfers from visiting Scotland. In fact, some golfers prefer the challenge of playing in severe weather conditions. Also, many Scottish courses have outstanding drainage systems, ensuring that even in rainy weather, the course is still playable.

Another crucial element to consider when organizing a golf trip to Scotland is where to stay. Scotland offers numerous superb hotels and resorts, some of which are located on or near famous golf courses. St Andrews is a popular location for golfers, and there are several hotels in the town that provide packages that include golf at the Old Course or other local courses. Other popular golf spots in Scotland include the Ayrshire Coast, East Lothian, and the Highlands.

When it comes to picking which courses to play, Scotland provides something for every level of golfer. In addition to the famed links courses, there are other parkland courses and heathland courses around the country. Some of the most notable parkland courses include Gleneagles, Lake Lomond, and The Carrick. Heathland courses, which are similar to parkland courses but with more heather and gorse, can be found in regions such as Fife and the Scottish Borders.

One of the distinctive elements of golfing in Scotland is the country's concept of "open" golf courses. Open courses are available to the public, meaning that anyone can play them for a price. This allows golfers to enjoy some of the most famous courses in the world, such as St Andrews Old Course, without becoming a member of a private club. However, it's crucial to realize that some open courses have rigorous rules and regulations, such as clothing codes and handicap requirements, so it's necessary to do research before booking a tee time.

Overall, golfing in Scotland offers an exceptional experience for golfers of all levels. With its magnificent courses, unique difficulties, and rich history and culture, Scotland is certainly a golfer's paradise. Whether you're a seasoned pro or a beginner, there's something for everyone to enjoy on Scotland's links courses and beyond.

Dialects and Language

Scotland is a country with a rich linguistic legacy, where different dialects and languages have been spoken over the centuries. The diversity of language in Scotland reflects the country's long and complex history, which has experienced numerous impacts from neighboring countries and invaders. In this section, we will investigate the dialects and languages of Scotland, their beginnings, and how they have evolved over time.

The predominant language spoken in Scotland is English, however, Scots is officially recognized as the official language of the country. Scots is a Germanic language that developed from Old English and was spoken in Scotland before the advent of the Normans in 1066. It was spoken by the majority of the population until the 15th century when English began to take hold. Scots is still spoken in several regions of Scotland, particularly in the Lowlands, and has affected Scottish English.

Another language spoken in Scotland is Gaelic, a Celtic language that originated in Ireland and was carried to Scotland by settlers in the 4th century AD. Gaelic was the main language in Scotland until the 15th century when it began to wane due to the impact of English. Nowadays, Gaelic is used by a minority of the population, especially in the Western Islands, and efforts have been made to restore the language and promote its use.

There are also several dialects of English spoken in Scotland. They include Scottish Standard English, which is the official version of English used in Scotland, and several regional dialects such as Doric in the Northeast, Lallans in the Lowlands, and Shetlandic in the Shetland Islands. These dialects have diverse characteristics in terms of pronunciation, vocabulary, and grammar, and reflect the diversity of Scottish culture and history.

The Scottish Standard English dialect is comparable to standard British English, but with minor variances in pronunciation and vocabulary. For example, the Scottish accent uses specific words and phrases that are not widely used in other parts of the UK, such as "wee" for small or "ken". There are additional variances in pronunciation, such as the rolling of the "r" sound in words like "car" and "bird".

Doric is a dialect spoken in the Northeast of Scotland, mainly in Aberdeenshire and Angus. It is defined by its peculiar pronunciation, which contains a high accent on the "ch" sound and a tendency to lose the "g" sound at the end of syllables. Vocabulary in Doric also differentiates from other dialects, with terms such as "foon" for phone and "scunnered" for fed up.

Lallans, sometimes known as Lowland Scots, is a dialect spoken in the Lowlands of Scotland, mainly in Edinburgh and Glasgow. Lallans is influenced by both Scots and English and has a distinct lexicon and pronunciation. For example, the Lallans dialect uses the word "auld" for old and "haud" for hold.

Shetlandic is a dialect spoken in the Shetland Islands, which are located in the North Sea, off the coast of mainland Scotland. Shetlandic has strong Norse influences and is defined by its peculiar pronunciation, which includes the usage of the "u" sound in terms like "fush" for fish and "buik" for book. Vocabulary in Shetlandic also differs from other dialects, including terms such as "haaf" for sea and "peerie" for little.

In conclusion, Scotland is a country with a rich linguistic legacy, where many dialects and languages have been spoken over the centuries. Scots and Gaelic are recognized as the official languages of the country, while several variants of English are also spoken. Some dialects have significant characteristics in terms of pronunciation, vocabulary,

Weather

The weather in Scotland can be classified as temperate and oceanic, indicating that it is often moderate, wet, and windy. Yet, due to its location in the north of Europe, Scotland can experience a wide range of weather conditions throughout the year, ranging from bright and sunny days to cold and snowy winters.

Summer in Scotland normally lasts from June through August and is considered the finest season to visit the nation. During this time, the weather is often pleasant and sunny, with average temperatures ranging from 15°C to 19°C (59°F to 66°F). However, it is crucial to understand that even during the summer months, Scotland can see periodic spells of rain and cloud cover, so it is best to be prepared for all weather conditions.

Autumn in Scotland, which runs from September through November, is characterized by lower weather, shorter days, and changing foliage. During this time, average temperatures range from 7°C to 14°C (45°F to 57°F), and rainfall increases. While the weather in autumn can be rather unpredictable, it is a perfect season to visit Scotland for individuals who prefer outdoor activities such as hiking and cycling.

Winter in Scotland, from December through February, is generally chilly and damp, with occasional precipitation. Typical temperatures during this period range from 2°C to 7°C (36°F to 45°F), although temperatures sometimes drop below freezing, particularly in the Highlands. While winter weather can be unpredictable, it is still a popular time to visit Scotland, particularly for people interested in skiing and other winter sports.

Spring in Scotland, from March to May, is characterized by milder temperatures, longer days, and blooming flowers. During this time, typical temperatures range from 6°C to 12°C (43°F to 54°F), although it is not uncommon for the weather to be colder or warmer than this. While spring might be a great time to visit Scotland, it is vital to be prepared for the occasional rain shower, as rainfall is typical throughout the year.

It is crucial to know that the weather in Scotland can vary drastically depending on where you are in the country. The west coast of Scotland, for example, tends to be wetter and milder than the east coast, while the Highlands suffer cooler temperatures and more snowfall than other sections of the country.

Overall, the weather in Scotland might be unpredictable, but by being prepared and flexible, visitors can enjoy everything that the nation has to offer regardless of the conditions. It is usually a good idea to check the weather forecast before visiting and to prepare accordingly for all weather conditions, including waterproof clothing and sturdy walking shoes.

In conclusion, Scotland's weather is temperate and oceanic, and while it can be unexpected, it is not as extreme as some other places in the world. Each season in Scotland has its own unique weather patterns and attractions, and tourists should prepare appropriately to make the most of their vacation. With its gorgeous landscapes, intriguing history, and vibrant culture, Scotland is a location that is well worth experiencing, regardless of the weather.

Getting Here

Traveling to Scotland is pretty easy, with various methods accessible, including air, sea, and land transportation. In this section, we will explore each means of transportation and offer you all the information you need to organize your trip to Scotland.

Air Transportation

Flying is the shortest way to get to Scotland. The country has five international airports, including Edinburgh Airport, Glasgow Airport, Aberdeen Airport, Inverness Airport, and Prestwick Airport. The majority of flights to Scotland are through Edinburgh and Glasgow airports, which are well-connected to major cities in Europe, North America, and Asia.

If you are traveling from North America, you can choose from a range of direct flights to Scotland. Airlines such as Delta, United, American Airlines, and British Airways offer direct flights from New York, Boston, Washington DC, and other important cities in the USA. Similarly, airlines such as Air Canada and WestJet offer direct flights from Canada. If you are flying from Europe, there are numerous direct flights from places such as Amsterdam, Paris, and Frankfurt.

If you are going from Asia, you can choose from a choice of airlines that offer connecting flights to Scotland. Airlines such as Emirates, Qatar Airways, and Etihad Airways offer connecting flights from places such as Dubai, Abu Dhabi, and Doha.

Sea Transportation

Another alternative to get to Scotland is by boat. Scotland has a number of ports that receive ferries from other nations. These ports include Aberdeen, Cairnryan, Dundee, Edinburgh, and Glasgow.

Ferries from Ireland and Northern Ireland connected to the ports of Cairnryan, Stranraer, and Troon. Similarly, ferries from Belgium and the Netherlands connected to the ports of Rosyth and Zeebrugge. If you are traveling from Scandinavia, ferries from Norway, Sweden, and Denmark connect to the ports of Aberdeen, Lerwick, and Kirkwall.

Land Transportation

If you are traveling from England, you can use the road and rail networks to get to Scotland. There are numerous direct rail routes from cities such as London, Manchester, and Birmingham to important Scottish cities such as Edinburgh and Glasgow. The journey time by train from London to Edinburgh is roughly 4.5 hours.

Similarly, there are various bus companies that run routes from England to Scotland. The journey time by bus is slightly longer than by train, but it is a cheaper choice. Additionally, if you are driving, you can travel the motorways and A-roads that connect Scotland with England.

Top Attractions

Scotland is famed for its rich cultural legacy, with a long history reaching back thousands of years. As a result, the country is home to a diverse range of cultural sites that provide visitors with a unique glimpse into Scottish culture, art, and traditions. From ancient monuments to modern museums, there is enough to see and do in Scotland for anyone interested in its rich cultural legacy. Following are some of the cultural attractions:

Edinburgh Castle

Edinburgh Castle is a historic fortification perched on top of Castle Rock, an extinct volcanic rock structure in the center of Edinburgh, Scotland. The castle has a long and fascinating history reaching back to the 12th century, and it has functioned as a royal palace, military stronghold, and national emblem for Scotland.

One of the most famous aspects of Edinburgh Castle is the Great Hall, a vast banquet hall erected in the 16th century by James IV. The hall is noteworthy for its elaborate timber roof and intricate tapestries, which depict incidents from Scottish history. Visitors can also explore the Crown Chamber, which holds the Scottish Crown Jewels, including the famed Stone of Destiny, a symbol of Scottish sovereignty.

Another popular sight at Edinburgh Castle is the Royal Palace, which was previously home to Scottish rulers such as Mary Queen of Scots and James VI. The palace has magnificent halls and chambers, notably the Queen's bedchamber and the King's bedchamber, which are adorned with costly furnishings and artwork.

For history aficionados, Edinburgh Castle also offers an insight into Scotland's military past. The castle has been the location of countless fights and sieges throughout its history, and tourists can examine the castle's military buildings and defenses, such as the Half-Moon Battery and the Argyle Battery. The castle's Military Museum is also worth a visit since it displays a collection of weaponry, uniforms, and items from Scotland's military history.

Apart from its historical significance, Edinburgh Castle also offers stunning views of the city of Edinburgh and its surroundings. Visitors may take in panoramic views of the city from the castle's walls and battlements, and on a clear day, they can see as far as the Firth of Forth and the Pentland Hills.

It is also home to various cultural events throughout the year, including the world-famous Edinburgh Military Tattoo, a spectacular display of military song, dance, and spectacle performed by the British Armed Forces and international military bands. The castle regularly holds concerts, exhibitions, and other cultural events that showcase Scottish tradition and culture.

Edinburgh Castle is also an essential emblem of Scottish identity and nationalism. The castle has played a key part in Scottish history and is regarded as a national landmark by many Scots. Its unique silhouette is instantly identifiable and has become linked with the city of Edinburgh and the country of Scotland.

Edinburgh Castle is a must-see site for anybody visiting Edinburgh, Scotland. The castle's rich history, spectacular architecture, and cultural significance make it one of the most popular tourist sites in Scotland. Visitors can tour the castle's many attractions, including the Great Hall, the Royal House, and the Military Museum, while also taking in the stunning views of the city from the castle's towers.

The Royal Mile

The Royal Mile is a historical and cultural core of Edinburgh. It spans approximately one mile from Edinburgh Castle to the Palace of Holyroodhouse and is a popular tourist site that is rich in history and culture. In this section, we will explore the numerous sites and attractions along the Royal Mile, as well as the history and significance of this historic boulevard.

The Royal Mile is noted for its spectacular architecture and its many historic structures, including St Giles' Cathedral, the Scottish Parliament, and the Museum of Edinburgh. The street is also home to a variety of stores, restaurants, and pubs, making it a fantastic destination for both tourists and locals.

Towards the bottom of the Royal Mile stands the Palace of Holyroodhouse, the former residence of the British king in Scotland. The palace has been the home of numerous monarchs throughout history, and tourists can take a tour of the state rooms and learn about the castle's interesting history.

Another must-see item on the Royal Mile is St Giles' Cathedral, which dates back to the 12th century. The cathedral is noted for its spectacular design and its rich history, having played a vital part in Scotland's religious and political life over the centuries. Visitors can take a tour of the cathedral and learn about its many fascinating features, including its stained-glass windows and its remarkable organ.

The Royal Mile is also home to a variety of other attractions, including the Scottish Parliament, the Museum of Edinburgh, and the Scotch Whisky Experience. The Scottish Parliament building is a modern architectural masterpiece, while the Museum of Edinburgh offers tourists a fascinating view of the city's history and culture. The Scotch Whisky Experience, meantime, is a must-visit for anyone interested in Scotland's famous whisky business.

Among its various attractions, the Royal Mile also has a rich and fascinating history. The street was previously a lively marketplace and the principal route in Edinburgh's ancient Old Town. During the decades, it became a prominent center of governance, religion, and culture, with many of its structures and sites dating back hundreds of years.

Today, the Royal Mile remains a significant element of Edinburgh's cultural scene, attracting millions of people from across the world each year. Whether you're interested in history, and architecture, or simply experiencing the sights and sounds of one of Scotland's most famous streets, there's something for everyone on the Royal Mile.

Its various attractions, rich history, and gorgeous architecture make it one of the most popular tourist sites in the country. Whether you're interested in visiting its many old buildings, sipping some of Scotland's famed whisky, or simply soaking up the ambiance of this bustling and historic street, the Royal Mile is a genuinely remarkable experience.

The Royal Botanic Garden Edinburgh

The Royal Botanic Garden Edinburgh is a world-renowned garden that encompasses an area of 70 acres and is home to approximately 13,000 plant varieties from throughout the world. The garden was built in 1670 as a physic garden to supply therapeutic plants for the University of Edinburgh. Over the years, it has developed to become one of the most important institutions for plant study and conservation in the world.

The garden is separated into numerous distinct parts, each with its own unique characteristics and flora. The most famous area is the Rock Garden, which was constructed in 1871 and displays a collection of alpine plants from throughout the world. The garden also features a collection of Scottish species, including heather, bluebells, and thistles, in the Scottish Heath Garden.

Another famous component is the Victorian Palm House, which was built in 1858 and is home to a collection of tropical and subtropical plants from throughout the world. The Palm House is a remarkable example of Victorian glasshouse construction, and its towering palms and exotic flora offer a really immersive tropical atmosphere.

The Royal Botanic Garden Edinburgh also plays a crucial role in plant conservation and research. The park is home to the Centre for Plant Diversity and Systematics, which holds one of the greatest herbarium collections in the world. The herbarium has nearly 3 million plant specimens, collected from all around the world, and is a great resource for scholars and scientists.

The garden is also home to the Edinburgh Biomes project, which intends to develop a network of world-class glasshouses to host some of the world's most endangered plants. The first of these biomes, the Temperate Palm House, debuted in 2021 and is home to a collection of flora from the Mediterranean, South Africa, and Australia.

For visitors, the Royal Botanic Garden Edinburgh offers a unique opportunity to explore the world of plants and learn about their critical role in our environment. The garden is open year-round and offers a number of events and activities, including guided tours, seminars, and exhibitions.

One of the most popular events is the Garden's annual Christmas light show, which transforms the garden into a dazzling world of light and color. Guests can explore the lit trails, enjoy live music, and warm up with a hot drink and a snack in the Garden's café.

For families with children, the garden offers a number of activities and events, including nature trails, storytelling sessions, and craft workshops. The garden's teaching program is aimed to develop a love of the environment and encourage young people to explore the natural world around them.

The Royal Botanic Garden Edinburgh is a must-visit location for anybody interested in flora, wildlife, and conservation. Its rich collections, world-class research facilities, and magnificent gardens make it a genuinely unique and valuable resource for visitors and scientists alike.

The Scottish National Gallery

The Scottish National Gallery, located in the center of Edinburgh, is one of the most prominent art museums in Scotland. It houses a great collection of Scottish and worldwide art, extending from the Renaissance to the 20th century. The gallery's collection is notably rich in the areas of Scottish art, Impressionism, and Post-Impressionism.

The Scottish National Gallery was formed in 1859 when the Scottish Academy acquired a facility on The Mound in Edinburgh to display its collection of artworks. Over the years, the collection grew through donations, bequests, and purchases, and the gallery expanded into adjacent buildings to accommodate the growing collection. Nowadays, the gallery has many interconnected structures, including the original 19th-century building, which now houses the Scottish Collection, and the 20th-century Royal Scottish Academy building, which holds the international collection.

The Scottish Collection is the center of the gallery's collection, and it comprises works by several of Scotland's most prominent artists, including Sir Henry Raeburn, Sir David Wilkie, Samuel John Peploe, and Joan Eardley. The collection also includes works by international painters who worked in Scotland or were inspired by Scottish themes, such as J.M.W. Turner and Paul Gauguin. Some of the highlights of the Scottish Collection are Raeburn's painting of The Reverend Robert Walker Skating on Duddingston Lake, Wilkie's The Penny Wedding, and Peploe's Still Life with Coffee Pot.

The foreign collection is also an important element of the Scottish National Gallery's assets, and it includes works by many of the most prominent artists of the Western heritage, from the Renaissance to the 20th century. The collection is notably rich in the genres of Impressionism and Post-Impressionism, and it contains works by painters such as Van Gogh, Monet, Cézanne, and Degas. Among the highlights of the international collection are Van Gogh's Sunflowers,

Monet's Water Lilies, and Cézanne's Les Grandes Baigneuses.

The Scottish National Gallery also presents a schedule of temporary exhibits throughout the year, which display works from the gallery's collection as well as loans from other museums and private collections. Previous exhibitions have featured shows on the work of Joan Eardley, Cut & Paste: 400 Years of Collage, and True to Life: British Realist Painting in the 1920s and 1930s.

The Scottish National Gallery offers a range of educational programs and events for visitors of all ages. They include guided tours, presentations, workshops, and family activities, as well as online resources like podcasts and virtual tours. The gallery's education initiatives strive to make art accessible and interesting for all visitors and to develop an understanding of the visual arts as an essential element of Scotland's cultural history.

The Scottish National Gallery is a must-visit place for every art fan visiting Scotland. Its collection of Scottish and foreign art is a monument to the richness and diversity of the aesthetic traditions of Scotland and the larger Western tradition. Its program of temporary exhibitions and educational programs ensures that there is always something new to discover at the gallery, and its central location in Edinburgh makes it easily accessible to people from all over the world.

Glasgow Cathedral

Glasgow Cathedral is a majestic and historically significant edifice located in the center of Glasgow. It is also known as the High Kirk of Glasgow or St. Mungo's Cathedral, named for the city's patron saint. The cathedral is one of the most important and finest examples of medieval architecture in Scotland, and it is also the oldest building in Glasgow, with elements of the construction dating back to the 12th century.

The cathedral was built on the place where St. Mungo, the founder of Glasgow, was said to have built his church in the 6th century. The present edifice was started in the 12th century, with the choir and crypt being the earliest elements of the church. During the ages, the cathedral was expanded and remodeled, with additions such as the Lady Chapel, which was built in the 15th century, and the exquisite stained glass windows, which were installed in the 19th century.

One of the most outstanding characteristics of the cathedral is its Gothic design, with soaring arches, elaborate stone carvings, and stunning stained glass windows. The cathedral's spire, which rises to a height of over 200 feet, is a prominent element of Glasgow's skyline and can be seen from miles away.

The cathedral is also home to a number of interesting historical items, notably the tomb of St. Mungo, which is placed in the crypt. The cathedral also houses the Blackadder Aisle, which is the final resting place of various prominent Scottish luminaries, including the philosopher John Napier and the physician William Hunter.

In addition to its historical significance, the cathedral is also an important place of worship, with regular services being held throughout the year. Guests are welcome to attend these services, as well as to explore the cathedral and its numerous treasures.

One of the most stunning parts of the cathedral is its stained glass windows, which are among the finest in Scotland. These windows portray scenes from the Bible and from Scottish history, and they are a monument to the skill and craftsmanship of the craftsmen who built them.

Visitors to the cathedral can also observe the stunning architecture and unique stone carvings that adorn the edifice. The cathedral's many chapels and alcoves are packed with intricate decorations and works of art, creating a serene and reflective atmosphere that is suitable for contemplation and prayer.

For those interested in history, the cathedral also provides a number of guided tours, which provide a fascinating insight into the building's past and its many treasures. These tours take tourists into the cathedral's many chapels and crypts, as well as allow an opportunity to explore the cathedral's amazing collection of artifacts and works of art.

Whether you are interested in history, and architecture, or simply in touring one of Scotland's most beautiful and historic buildings, the cathedral is guaranteed to captivate and inspire you. With its soaring arches, elaborate stone carvings, and exquisite stained glass windows, the cathedral is a tribute to the skill and artistry of the craftsmen who made it, and it remains one of the most important and revered buildings in all of Scotland.

Stirling Castle

Stirling Castle is a historic stronghold located in the city of Stirling. The castle is one of the largest and most important castles in Scotland and has played a vital part in Scottish history since the 12th century. The castle is positioned atop Castle Hill, which overlooks the city of Stirling and the surrounding countryside, making it a perfect location for strategic military operations.

Stirling Castle has been the site of several notable events throughout history, including battles, sieges, and coronations. In fact, the castle was a major location throughout the Wars of Scottish Independence in the late 13th and early 14th centuries, with multiple engagements being fought in and around the fortress. The most famous of these confrontations was the Battle of Stirling Bridge in 1297, where Scottish soldiers under the command of William Wallace destroyed a far larger English army. This victory marked a turning moment in the war and is widely commemorated in Scotland to this day.

Stirling Castle has also been the venue of countless coronations throughout history. Arguably the most notable of these was the coronation of Mary, Queen of Scots in 1543. Mary was just nine months old at the time, and her coronation was an attempt to secure the Scottish crown for the Stuart dynasty. The event took place in the castle's Chapel Royal, which is still one of the most impressive features of the castle today.

Today, Stirling Castle is one of Scotland's most prominent tourist sites, drawing tourists from around the world to enjoy its rich history and breathtaking architecture. The castle has been significantly repaired and refurbished in recent years, with many of its buildings and features going back to the 15th and 16th centuries. Guests can visit the castle's many halls and chambers, including the Great Hall, the Royal Palace, and the Queen Anne Garden, which was renovated in the 20th century.

One of the most distinctive elements of Stirling Castle is its architecture, which is a unique blend of medieval and Renaissance styles. The castle's Great Hall, for example, is a beautiful example of medieval construction, with its high oak ceiling and elaborate carvings. The Royal Palace, on the other hand, is a marvel of Renaissance design, with its exquisite windows and artistic façade.

Visitors to Stirling Castle can also enjoy spectacular views of the surrounding countryside from the castle's battlements, which give panoramic panoramas of the city and the adjoining hills. In addition, the castle is home to a number of intriguing exhibitions and displays, including a collection of weaponry and armor, and a display on the life and reign of Mary, Queen of Scots.

The castle's rich history, gorgeous architecture, and beautiful location make it a really unique and memorable tourist attraction. Whether you're interested in visiting the castle's various halls and chambers, taking in the stunning views from its battlements, or learning more about Scotland's rich history, Stirling Castle is guaranteed to impress and inspire visitors of all ages.

Culloden Battlefield

Culloden Battlefield is a historic site located in Inverness, that is famed for being the location of the final fight of the Jacobite rebellion of 1745. The fight was fought on April 16, 1746, and was the culmination of a rebellion by the Scottish highlanders, who were aiming to restore the Stuart monarchy to the British crown. The fight is considered to be one of the most significant episodes in Scottish history, and the location is now a popular attraction for visitors and history aficionados.

The Battle of Culloden was fought between the Jacobite troops, led by Prince Charles Edward Stuart, and the British government forces, led by the Duke of Cumberland. The Jacobites were mostly made up of Scottish highlanders, who were fiercely committed to the Stuart cause and had fought for it in past rebellions. The government forces, on the other hand, were made up of soldiers from England, Scotland, and Ireland, and were well-trained and well-equipped.

The battle took place on a moorland area known as Culloden Moor, which is now part of the Culloden Battlefield site. The battlefield is situated 12 miles east of Inverness and encompasses an area of nearly 1.5 square miles. The site features a tourist center, which provides information about the war and the events leading up to it, as well as a memorial cairn, which was created in 1881 to memorialize those who died in the battle.

Visitors to the Culloden Battlefield can explore the site and learn about the history of the fight through a choice of exhibitions and displays. The visitor center has a huge collection of relics and interactive displays that provide insight into the events leading up to the conflict, as well as the battle itself. Visitors can also view a film that recreates the conflict, giving them a taste of what it would have been like to have been there.

The battlefield site itself is also home to a number of interesting features and landmarks. One of the most noteworthy of these is the Clan Stone, which is a tribute to the clans who fought on the Jacobite side in the conflict. The stone contains the names of the clans and their individual chiefs and is a sad reminder of the human cost of the struggle.

Another noteworthy element of the battlefield site is the monument cairn, which sits on the point where the government soldiers started their attack on the Jacobite lines. The cairn is a massive, circular construction formed of local stones, and has a plaque that commemorates the names of the government soldiers who died in combat. The cairn is a striking reminder of the human toll of the struggle and serves as a symbol of the sacrifice made by those who fought on both sides.

The site is well-preserved and well-maintained and provides visitors with a choice of possibilities to learn about the history of the conflict and the events that led up to it. Whether you are a history enthusiast or simply curious about this crucial moment in Scottish history, a visit to the Culloden Battlefield is well worth the trip.

The National Museum of Scotland

The National Museum of Scotland is an outstanding cultural institution located in Edinburgh. The museum, which opened in 2011, is one of the most visited destinations in the country and provides tourists with a comprehensive collection of items and exhibits that represent Scotland's history, culture, and natural heritage.

The museum's structure itself is an amazing work of architecture, with a modern design that integrates harmoniously with the surrounding historic buildings. The museum is situated across multiple floors, each dedicated to a unique theme or historical period, and gives visitors a wealth of information and interactive displays that make learning about Scotland's past and present both interesting and instructive.

The displays at the National Museum of Scotland include a wide range of topics, from prehistoric Scotland and the Roman invasion through the Scottish Enlightenment and the Industrial Revolution. Visitors can learn about the country's rich history of art, design, and invention, as well as its natural legacy, including its distinct geology, vegetation, and fauna.

One of the attractions of the museum is the Grand Gallery, a stunning area that shows the museum's most prominent objects, including the world-renowned Lewis chess pieces, which date back to the 12th century. The exhibition also contains a selection of interactive displays, including a virtual reality experience that allows visitors to explore the Scottish environment in amazing detail.

Other prominent displays include the Exploring Scotland gallery, which provides visitors with an interactive trip through Scotland's past and present, from the Stone Age to the current day. The gallery offers a mix of relics and interactive displays, including a recreated Iron Age roundhouse, a Viking longship, and a reproduction of a 19th-century New Town street.

The museum also features numerous galleries dedicated to Scotland's artistic and design heritage, including the Art and Design gallery, which showcases a range of works by Scottish artists and designers, from traditional tartan to modern fashion and textiles. The Fashion and Style gallery, meanwhile, covers Scotland's significance in the evolution of fashion and design, with exhibits spanning from 18th-century gowns to present streetwear.

In addition to its permanent displays, the National Museum of Scotland also organizes a selection of temporary exhibitions throughout the year. These exhibitions cover a wide range of topics, from the history of Scottish music to the work of current artists, and allow visitors the chance to explore a diverse collection of objects and artworks.

For visitors interested in learning more about Scotland's natural heritage, the museum's Natural World galleries provide a selection of exhibitions that illustrate the country's various landscapes, fauna, and geology. Attractions include a display of Scotland's prehistoric marine animals, a gallery dedicated to the country's spectacular shoreline, and a collection of specimens from Scotland's unique fauna, including red deer and golden eagles.

The Isle of Skye

The Isle of Skye is a stunning and breathtaking place located off the west coast. This island is noted for its rough scenery, stunning shoreline, and rich cultural legacy. The island has a rich and fascinating history, with signs of human settlement extending back to the ancient age. Today, Skye is a famous tourist destination, allowing visitors the chance to see its natural beauty, learn about its history and culture, and enjoy a choice of outdoor sports.

One of the most distinctive qualities of Skye is its rocky, hilly topography. The island is dominated by the Cuillin mountain range, which has some of the most demanding and scenic peaks in the UK. The Black Cuillin is particularly famous, with its craggy peaks and high cliffs attracting climbers and hikers from throughout the world. Nonetheless, the island also offers gentler walks and climbs, with numerous magnificent routes flowing through the hills and glens.

Skye is also noted for its gorgeous beaches. The island's rough shoreline is filled with lovely bays, quiet coves, and stunning sea cliffs. One of the most recognized landmarks on the island is the Old Man of Storr, a towering rock structure that juts out from the surrounding hills. The Quiraing is another popular site, with its distinctive rock formations and beautiful views over the sea.

Skye is also home to a rich cultural legacy, with a long history of Gaelic language and culture. Visitors can learn about the island's history at a selection of museums and heritage sites, including the Skye Museum of Island Life and the Clan Donald Centre. The island is also home to a variety of old ruins, notably the famed Dunvegan Castle, which dates back to the 13th century.

One of the best ways to experience Skye's culture is through its traditional music and dancing. The island is noted for its traditional folk music, which is often played on the fiddle and bagpipes. Guests can enjoy live performances at local bars and cultural events throughout the year. Skye is also home to a variety of traditional ceilidhs, which are social gatherings when people join together to dance, sing, and enjoy music.

Skye is home to a multitude of native animals, including otters, seals, red deer, and golden eagles. Tourists can take boat cruises to observe dolphins and whales or go on guided hikes to discover rare birds and other creatures.

The Whisky Trail

The Whisky Trail is a popular tourist route that takes visitors through some of the country's most scenic landscapes, historic distilleries, and traditional Scottish pubs. The route travels through the Speyside region, which is recognized for producing some of the world's greatest whiskies.

The Speyside region is home to more than half of Scotland's distilleries, and The Whisky Trail is a terrific way to explore the area and learn more about the history and manufacture of Scotch whisky. The route starts in the village of Craigellachie, located in the heart of the Speyside region, and takes tourists through a range of distilleries, each with its own unique style and flavor.

One of the pleasures of The Whisky Trail is the opportunity to visit some of Scotland's most famous distilleries, including Glenfiddich, The Macallan, and Glenlivet. These distilleries offer tours that take guests through the full whisky-making process, from the malting of the barley to the ultimate maturing of the whisky in oak casks.

The Glenfiddich distillery, for example, is one of the oldest and most famous in Scotland. Guests can take a tour of the distillery and learn about the history of the brand, as well as the production process. The Macallan distillery, on the other hand, is famed for its unique technique of whisky-making, which involves utilizing only the finest sherry oak casks to age the whisky.

In addition to the distilleries, The Whisky Trail also takes travelers through some of Scotland's most scenic landscapes.

The trail travels through the Cairngorms National Park, which is home to some of Scotland's tallest mountains, as well as a variety of species, including red deer and golden eagles.

One of the most scenic parts of the trail is the journey between Glenlivet and Tomintoul, which brings visitors into the heart of the Speyside landscape. Along the journey, travelers can stop at traditional Scottish pubs and eat some of the native cuisine, including haggis, neeps, and tatties.

Another highlight of The Whisky Trail is the option to participate in tastings and masterclasses, where visitors may try a range of whiskies and learn about the different flavors and scents that make each one unique. The Speyside Whisky Academy, located in the town of Dufftown, offers a range of classes and tastings, as well as a whisky-themed restaurant.

Top Cuisine to Try Out

Another facet of Scottish culture that sometimes goes forgotten is its cuisine. Scotland's cuisine is greatly impacted by its climate and environment, which includes abundant agriculture. Let's discuss the distinct meals and components that makeup Scotland's cuisine.

Haggis

Haggis is a classic Scottish meal that has been a part of the country's culinary legacy for centuries. It is produced by blending sheep's organs, such as the heart, liver, and lungs, with onions, oats, spices, and stock. The combination is then enclosed in a sheep's stomach lining and cooked for several hours. Haggis is frequently served with neeps and tatties, which are mashed turnips and potatoes, respectively.

Haggis is a unique cuisine that has a particular flavor and texture. The organs provide the meal with a rich, meaty flavor, while the oats and spices lend a nutty and somewhat spicy flavor. The texture of haggis is comparable to that of sausage, with a little crumbly and gritty texture.

Haggis is a popular dish in Scotland and is commonly served at traditional Scottish festivals, such as Burns Night, which is held annually on January 25th. It is also a common dish in Scottish cuisine and can be found in many restaurants and pubs throughout the country.

Despite its popularity, haggis is a contentious dish, with some people finding the concept of eating sheep's organs unappetizing. Nonetheless, haggis is a sustainable and environmentally friendly food, as it makes use of components of the animal that would otherwise go to waste. Moreover, haggis is a high source of protein and important nutrients, making it a healthy choice for individuals who prefer meat.

There are several varieties of haggis, with some recipes containing additional ingredients like suet or whisky. Vegetarian varieties of haggis also exist, which replace beef with vegetables and pulses.

If you're planning a vacation to Scotland, trying haggis is a must-do activity. While it may sound daunting, many individuals discover that they appreciate the dish once they give it a try. It's a distinct and authentic flavor of Scottish cuisine that is not to be missed.

Cullen skink

Cullen skink is a traditional Scottish soup that originated in the seaside town of Cullen, located in the northeast part of Scotland. It is a substantial soup cooked with smoked haddock, potatoes, onions, and milk or cream. The dish is a popular comfort food in Scotland and is commonly served as a starter or main course in restaurants and cafés.

The soup's main ingredient, smoked haddock, is a species of fish that is fished in the North Sea and then smoked over oak chips. The smokey flavor of the haddock is what gives Cullen skink its characteristic flavor. The potatoes and onions are diced and cooked in a skillet with butter until they are soft and transparent. Finally, the smoked haddock is added to the pan along with enough water to cover the contents. The mixture is boiled for around 15 minutes until the fish is cooked through.

After the fish is cooked, it is removed from the pan and flaked into small pieces. The potatoes and onions are then mashed using a potato masher to make a rich and creamy basis for the soup. Milk or cream is added to the pan and cooked until it is just below boiling. The mashed potato and onion mixture is then added to the pan and stirred until it is completely mixed. Lastly, the flaking haddock is reintroduced back to the pan and gently cooked through.

Cullen skink is generally served with a bit of crusty bread or oatcakes on the side. The soup is rich and nourishing, making it the perfect comfort food on a cold Scottish day. It is also a fantastic way to use up leftover smoked haddock from a fish supper.

Whlle Cullen skink is a famous dish in Scotland, it may not be as well-known to foreigners. Yet, it is worth attempting if you have the opportunity to do so. The smokey flavor of the haddock mixed with the creamy potato and onion base is a great combo. Additionally, it is a terrific way to enjoy traditional Scottish cuisine and culture. Whether you are dining at a neighborhood restaurant or cooking it at home, Cullen skink is guaranteed to be a fulfilling and tasty dish.

Scotch broth

Scotch broth is a classic Scottish soup that is often cooked with lamb or mutton, barley, and a variety of vegetables. The soup has been a mainstay in Scottish cuisine for generations and is considered a comfort food by many people.

The base of the Scotch broth is commonly produced by boiling lamb or mutton bones with vegetables such as onions, carrots, and leeks for several hours. This generates a rich, delicious broth that forms the foundation of the soup. The meat is then removed from the bones and placed back into the soup along with pearl barley and other vegetables including turnips, potatoes, and celery. The soup is seasoned with salt, pepper, and sometimes thyme or other herbs.

Scotch broth is a rich, nourishing soup that is commonly consumed as a main meal. It is often served with bread or oatcakes and is a popular dish throughout the colder months of the year. The soup is also regularly served at Scottish gatherings and events such as Hogmanay (New Year's Eve) and Burns Night (celebrating the life and works of poet Robert Burns).

One of the primary elements of Scotch broth is barley, which is a healthy grain that is high in fiber, protein, and vitamins. The grain is often used in traditional Scottish cuisine and is considered a staple meal in the country.

In addition to being a wonderful and substantial supper, Scotch broth has also been associated with many health advantages. The soup provides a wonderful source of vitamins and minerals, including iron, zinc, and vitamin B12, which are crucial for maintaining a strong immune system and preventing anemia. The soup is also a rich source of protein and fiber, which can aid with weight management and digestion.

Stovies

This hearty and nourishing dish is produced from simple ingredients, often comprising slow-cooked pork, potatoes, onions, and beef stock. While there are variations of stovies throughout Scotland, the meal is usually regarded as a mainstay of Scottish cuisine.

Stovies are commonly made using leftovers from a Sunday roast, with the meat shredded or diced into small bits before being put into the saucepan. The potatoes are also frequently cut or diced into little bits, which enables them to break down while boiling and thickening the stew. The onions are normally coarsely chopped and added to the saucepan alongside the meat and potatoes.

Once the ingredients are in the pot, they are covered with beef stock and simmered slowly over low heat for several hours. This slow cooking procedure allows the tastes of the ingredients to merge together, resulting in a rich and flavorful stew that is excellent for cold winter nights.

Other variations of stovies include the addition of other vegetables such as carrots or turnips, as well as herbs and spices such as thyme or bay leaves. Some recipes also call for the use of a dash of vinegar, which helps to tenderize the meat and lend a tangy flavor to the dish.

Stovies are generally served with a side of bread or oatcakes, which are great for mopping up the rich gravy. The meal is also typically served with pickled onions or beets, which help to cut through the richness of the stew.

While stovies are a traditional Scottish meal, they are still appreciated by residents and visitors alike. Several pubs and restaurants in Scotland serve stovies as a hearty and comforting supper, and it is also a popular dish to make at home for family gatherings or special events.

With their basic ingredients and slow cooking technique, they are the perfect dinner for cold winter nights and are sure to warm the heart and spirit of anyone who tries them.

Cranachan

Cranachan is a great blend of sweet, tangy, and creamy flavors. It is frequently offered for special occasions like weddings, birthdays, or Burns Night, a celebration of the famed Scottish poet Robert Burns. Cranachan is an easy dish to create, and it only requires a few basic ingredients.

The main ingredients of Cranachan include whipped cream, honey, oats, and fresh raspberries. Sometimes, Scottish whiskey is also added to give the dish a smokey flavor. The dish is normally prepared by softly toasting the oats in a dry frying pan until they get golden brown. Finally, the oats are combined with a small bit of honey and set aside to cool. Meanwhile, the raspberries are rinsed and left aside.

The next step is to whisk the cream until it forms stiff peaks. Once the cream is whipped, the cooled oats are incorporated into the cream along with a small splash of whisky (optional) to give the dessert a sense of smokiness. Finally, the dessert is created by stacking the whipped cream and oat mixture with fresh raspberries. The dessert can be served immediately, or it can be cooled in the fridge for a few hours before serving.

Cranachan has a long history in Scotland, and it is thought to have originated in the Scottish Highlands. Historically, Cranachan was made with crowdie, a Scottish cheese formed from curdled milk. Nevertheless, as time went on, whipped cream became a more popular addition to the dish, and it finally replaced the cheese.

Cranachan is a dessert that is strongly ingrained in Scottish culture, and it is commonly offered during important events. It is a simple yet tasty delicacy that emphasizes the natural flavors of the Scottish environment. The oats and raspberries used in the dessert are both classics of Scottish cuisine, and the honey used to sweeten the dish is often supplied by local beekeepers.

Cranachan is a dessert that genuinely depicts the natural flavors of Scotland, and it is a cuisine that is strongly rooted in Scottish tradition.

Bannock

Bannock is a sort of bread that has been a traditional component in Scottish cuisine for centuries. It is a simple, flatbread that can be created with just a few basic components, such as flour, baking soda, salt, and milk or water. Bannock is quick to cook, easy to store, and is a fantastic snack or lunch for travelers and visitors who are visiting the Scottish countryside.

The history of bannock in Scotland stretches back to the days of the Celtic, who used to produce a similar form of bread from oats and barley. Once wheat became more commonly available in Scotland, the recipe for bannock changed to include wheat flour, and it has been a popular food ever since. In fact, bannock is so closely connected with Scottish culture that it is often referred to as "Scotch bread."

There are several different variants of bannock that are popular in different regions of Scotland. For example, in the Highlands, bannock is often prepared with oats and is called an "oatcake." In different parts of Scotland, bannock may be cooked with potatoes or even fish, depending on the local ingredients and customs.

One of the beautiful things about bannock is that it is quite versatile and can be consumed in many different ways. It can be served hot or cold, with sweet or savory toppings, and can even be used as a base for sandwiches. Some popular toppings for bannock include butter, jam, honey, cheese, and smoked salmon.

Bannock is also an excellent food for travelers and tourists, as it is easy to pack and can be consumed on the go. It is widely loved by hikers and campers who require a quick and hearty lunch when out in the Scottish outdoors.

In recent years, bannock has also become more popular as a gourmet cuisine item in restaurants and cafes around Scotland. Chefs have experimented with different ingredients and techniques to create new and unique variations of this classic dish, and it is now possible to get bannock that has been seasoned with everything from wild berries to whisky.

Black pudding

Black pudding, a sort of blood sausage, is a favorite morning meal. It is created using pig's blood, oats, and spices, which are combined together and then put into a casing. The mixture is then cooked until it is firm and slices of black pudding can be served hot or cold, commonly accompanied by other breakfast foods such as eggs, bacon, and toast.

Although black pudding is frequently enjoyed throughout the United Kingdom, the Scottish variation has a particular flavor and texture that distinguishes it from other forms of blood sausage. The addition of oats gives Scottish black pudding a slightly nutty flavor, while the spices used in the mixture, such as allspice, nutmeg, and cloves, offer a warm and aromatic aspect.

In Scotland, black pudding has a long history and is considered a traditional meal. It is often eaten as part of a complete Scottish breakfast, which normally includes bacon, sausage, eggs, mushrooms, and baked beans. Some Scots also love black pudding as a snack, served cold with a splash of mustard.

In recent years, Scottish black pudding has acquired prominence as a gourmet element in restaurants and as an export commodity. Chefs utilize it in a range of recipes, such as black pudding-stuffed chicken breasts or black pudding and apple tarts. Scottish black pudding has also been recognized with accolades, such as the Great Taste Award, which is granted to great food and drink items in the UK.

Despite its popularity, the black pudding may be a polarizing cuisine, with some individuals finding the concept of swallowing blood unappetizing. Nonetheless, for many Scots, black pudding is an intrinsic part of their culinary heritage and a great accompaniment to any breakfast or dinner.

While others may find the concept of swallowing blood unappetizing, for many Scots, black pudding is a valued part of their culinary tradition.

Neeps and tatties

Neeps and tatties are meals that are immensely loved among locals and visitors alike. Neeps and tatties are essentially turnips and potatoes, respectively, and are typically served as a side dish to accompany a main course. The meal is simple yet hearty, and its origins may be traced back to Scotland's agricultural traditions.

Neeps, or turnips, are a root vegetable that is widely grown in Scotland. They have a slightly sweet and earthy taste and are typically used in stews, soups, and casseroles. In neeps and tatties, the turnips are boiled and mashed, generally with a big dollop of butter or cream. This gives the meal a rich and creamy texture that nicely matches the flavors of the turnips.

Tatties, or potatoes, are another staple of Scottish cuisine. Potatoes were introduced to Scotland in the late 16th century, and they immediately became a popular crop due to their adaptability and ability to grow in the Scottish environment. In neeps and tatties, the potatoes are boiled and mashed with butter and milk to achieve a smooth and creamy texture.

Neeps and tatties are traditionally served with haggis, a delicious pudding prepared from sheep's heart, liver, and lungs, combined with onions, spices, and oats. Haggis, neeps, and tatties comprise the legendary Scottish dish known as "haggis, neeps, and tatties," which is often served on Burns Night, a celebration of the life and works of Scottish poet Robert Burns.

For travelers visiting Scotland, trying neeps and tatties is a must-do experience. While the dish may seem basic, it is a true depiction of Scottish culture and heritage. Several restaurants and pubs in Scotland serve neeps and tatties as a side dish, therefore it is simple to find this meal on the menu.

If you want to really immerse yourself in Scottish culture, consider attending a Burns Night celebration, where you may savor haggis, neeps, and tatties while listening to poetry and music. Or, you can try making neeps and tatties yourself by following a traditional Scottish recipe. This may be an enjoyable and instructive event that allows you to learn more about Scottish cuisine and culture.

In conclusion, neeps and tatties are a delightful and simple Scottish dish that is a must-try for any traveler visiting Scotland. Whether eaten as a side dish or as part of the renowned haggis, neeps, and tatties supper, this dish is a true embodiment of Scottish culture and history. So, be sure to add neeps and tatties to your list of must-try Scottish delicacies!

Best Time To Visit

The weather is one of the most essential concerns when arranging a trip to Scotland. The country experiences a maritime climate, which implies that it is mild and damp throughout the year. However, the weather might vary greatly depending on the time of year and the place that you are visiting.

The summer months, from June through August, are typically regarded as the greatest time to visit Scotland. During this period, the weather is mild and pleasant, with typical temperatures ranging from 15°C to 20°C. The days are also long, with up to 17 hours of daylight in some parts of the nation, offering adequate time to explore the outdoors and enjoy outdoor activities like as hiking, cycling, and fishing.

Another reason why summer is the greatest time to visit Scotland is that numerous festivals and events take place during this time. The Edinburgh International Festival and the Royal Edinburgh Military Tattoo are two of the most popular events, bringing tourists from all over the world. The Highland Games, a series of traditional Scottish events, also take place during the summer months, providing a unique glimpse into Scottish culture and traditions.

Yet, summer is also the busiest time of year in Scotland, with many people flocking to the country to enjoy the beautiful weather and events. As a result, housing and transit can be more expensive, and famous destinations can be congested.

If you prefer quieter and less crowded areas, then spring and fall can also be ideal periods to visit Scotland. During these seasons, the weather is still warm, with average temperatures ranging from 10°C to 15°C. The days are also shorter than in summer, but there is still plenty of daylight to explore the outdoors.

Spring, in particular, is a terrific time to visit Scotland, as the countryside comes to life with vibrant flowers and trees blossoming. It is also an excellent time to view animals, as many species begin to emerge from hibernation.

Fall, on the other hand, is an excellent season to visit Scotland if you prefer outdoor activities such as hiking and cycling. The changing colors of the trees and surroundings give a wonderful backdrop for outdoor pursuits.

Winter is the least popular period to visit Scotland, due to the chilly and often wet weather. Yet, if you don't mind the weather, then winter may be a fantastic time to visit Scotland. The snow-capped mountains and frozen lochs create a stunning backdrop for winter activities such as skiing and snowboarding. The festive season, from late November to early January, is also an excellent time to visit Scotland, as many cities and towns are decorated with Christmas lights and decorations.

In short, the best time to visit Scotland depends on your choices and interests. If you prefer outdoor activities and festivals, then summer is the greatest season to visit. But, if you prefer quieter areas and appreciate wildlife and changing landscapes, then spring and fall can also be fantastic times to visit. Winter is the least popular time to visit Scotland, yet it can be a magnificent time for winter sports and Christmas celebrations. Ultimately, whenever you decide to visit Scotland, you are sure to be enthralled by its breathtaking landscapes, rich history, and vibrant culture.

Vacation Itinerary

A week-long trip to Scotland might be a fantastic way to discover some of the country's most recognizable sights and hidden wonders. In this section, we will present a thorough 1-week travel itinerary for Scotland that covers some of the most popular places in the country.

1 Week Vacation Itinerary

Day 1: Edinburgh

Start your Scottish vacation by exploring the ancient and bustling city of Edinburgh. Spend the day exploring the city's notable landmarks, such as Edinburgh Castle, the Royal Mile, and Holyrood Palace. Take a walk through the lovely Princes Street Gardens and climb to the summit of Arthur's Seat for breathtaking panoramic views of the city.

Day 2: Stirling and Loch Lomond

On day two, take a day trip to the lovely town of Stirling. Visit Stirling Castle, one of the largest and most important castles in Scotland, and the site of many key historical events. After exploring Stirling, head to adjacent Lake Lomond, the largest lake in Scotland. Enjoy a boat tour of the lake or explore one of the many trails around the area.

Day 3: Island of Skye

On day three, travel to the Isle of Skye, one of Scotland's most beautiful and secluded islands. Ride the ferry from Mallaig to Armadale and discover the island's rough shoreline, stunning mountains, and quaint settlements. Attractions include the Fairy Pools, Old Man of Storr, and the Cuillin Mountains.

Day 4: Inverness
Travel north to the city of Inverness regarded as the 'Gateway to the Highlands.' See the ancient Culloden Battlefield, the location of the last major combat fought on British soil, and learn about the Jacobite insurrection. Visit Inverness Castle and River Ness, or take a day trip to adjacent Loch Ness, home of the fabled Loch Ness Monster.

Day 5: Speyside
On day five, travel to Speyside. Tour some of the region's most famous distilleries, such as Glenfiddich, Macallan, and Balvenie, and learn about the history and creation of Scotland's national drink. Enjoy a whisky tasting and take in the scenic beauty of the surrounding area.

Day 6: Glasgow
Travel to Scotland's largest city, Glasgow, and spend the day touring its many museums, galleries, and cultural sites. Visit the Kelvingrove Art Gallery and Museum, the Riverside Museum, and the Glasgow Science Centre. Take a trip around the trendy West End district and experience some of the city's greatest shopping and cuisine.

Day 7: Lake Lomond and Trossachs National Park
On your final day, take a tour of Lake Lomond and the Trossachs National Park, one of Scotland's most spectacular natural places. Take a lovely drive through the park and stop at some of the many picturesque villages along the way. Enjoy a boat tour of Lake Katrine, or hike one of the many trails in the region.

With this itinerary, you may see some of the most recognizable places in Scotland while also uncovering hidden gems along the way.

2 weeks' Vacation Itinerary

With lots to explore and experience throughout the length of a two-week journey. Here is a proposed itinerary for a two-week trip to Scotland that covers some of the country's most popular sights and attractions.

Day 1-3: Edinburgh
Start your vacation in Edinburgh, and spend the first few days touring the city's ancient old town, including the magnificent Edinburgh Castle and the Royal Mile. Be sure to see the Palace of Holyroodhouse, and take a trip up to Arthur's Seat for spectacular views of the city.

Day 4-6: Glasgow
Taking a train or driving west to Glasgow, spend a few days seeing its thriving cultural scene, including the Kelvingrove Art Gallery and Museum, the Glasgow Science Centre, and the Glasgow Cathedral. Take a walk around the West End and see the eccentric shops and cafes on Ashton Lane.

Day 7-8: Lake Lomond
From Glasgow, go north to Loch Lomond. Take a boat tour out onto the loch, or trek one of the many trails around the loch for spectacular views of the surrounding mountains and farmland.

Day 9-10: Island of Skye
Catch a ferry from Mallaig to the Isle of Skye. Spend a few days visiting the island's many attractions, including the

beautiful Cuillin Mountains, the Quiraing rock formation, and the quaint fishing village of Portree.

Day 11-12: Inverness
From Skye, drive east to Inverness, take a walk along the River Ness, see Inverness Castle, and tour the city's many historic monuments, including the Culloden Battlefield and the Clava Cairns.

Day 13-14: Cairngorms National Park
Finish your tour by driving south to the Cairngorms National Park, Scotland's largest national park. Spend your final days touring the park's various attractions, including the Cairngorm Mountain Railway, the Highland Wildlife Park, and the magnificent Lake Morlich.

This trip delivers a nice mix of Scotland's urban and rural destinations, allowing travelers to enjoy the best of both worlds. While this itinerary includes some of Scotland's most popular attractions, there is still plenty to explore and discover in this wonderful country.

When organizing your trip, make sure to take into account the time of year you will be traveling. Scotland's weather can be unpredictable, so it is necessary to pack for all scenarios. Summer is the most popular time to visit Scotland, with longer days and warmer temperatures, but it is also the busiest and most expensive time of year. Spring and autumn might be quieter and more affordable, but the weather can be more unpredictable. Winter might be a lovely time to visit Scotland, with snowy vistas and comfortable pubs, but it can also be chilly and dark.

Another factor while organizing your trip is transportation. Scotland has a decent public transportation infrastructure, with trains and buses connecting most main sites, but hiring a car can provide more flexibility and allow travelers to explore more rural sections of the country.

This two-week schedule provides an excellent introduction to the country, but there is always more to learn and experience. Whether you are interested in history, culture, outdoor sports, or simply enjoying the beauty of the Scottish countryside, Scotland is a location that is guaranteed to leave a lasting impression.

Scotland On a Budget

With a plethora of intriguing things to see and do, it is no surprise that Scotland is a popular tourist destination. But, it is also true that Scotland can be an expensive location to visit, with accommodation, food, and attractions all piling up rapidly. That being said, with some careful planning and study, it is feasible to visit Scotland on a budget without compromising on your experience. In this section, we will discuss some excellent tips and tactics for visiting Scotland on a budget.

Schedule your visit wisely

The time of year you pick to visit Scotland might have a big impact on the expense of your vacation. Typically, the main tourist season in Scotland is during the summer months, from June through August. During this period, lodging prices are often higher, and famous tourist attractions can be more congested. If you are wanting to visit Scotland on a budget, consider traveling during the shoulder seasons, which are April to May and September to October. During these months, you will still have nice weather, but rates are frequently lower, and there are fewer tourists around.

Select budget-friendly accommodation

Accommodation is one of the major expenses when traveling, but there are various ways to save money. Hostels are a popular choice for budget-conscious tourists, with several options accessible throughout Scotland. Another economical choice is Airbnb, where you may rent a room or a full apartment, often at a quarter of the cost of a hotel. If you prefer the comfort of a hotel, seek budget-friendly businesses such as Premier Inn or Travelodge. Finally, consider camping, as Scotland has an abundance of campgrounds, and camping is a terrific way to explore the country's gorgeous scenery.

Take public transport

While renting a car may seem like the most convenient method to travel in Scotland, it may also be pricey. Alternatively, consider utilizing public transport, which is often much more economical. Scotland has an extensive network of buses and railways, which can take you to many major destinations. Also, traveling by rail is a fantastic chance to take in Scotland's gorgeous countryside. If you plan to use public transport regularly, consider obtaining a travel pass, such as the Scottish Explorer Pass, which permits unlimited travel on trains, buses, and ferries.

Plan your meals

Dining out can rapidly become a substantial expense when traveling. To save money, plan your meals in advance and consider cooking your food. Several hostels and Airbnb properties include common kitchens, allowing you to prepare meals at a lower cost than eating out. Moreover, look for budget-friendly dining options, such as street food or grocery dinners. Scotland is known for its fish and chips, haggis, and other traditional dishes, so make sure to try some of these budget-friendly options on your stay.

Take advantage of free attractions

Scotland provides a variety of free attractions, allowing you to enjoy the country's rich history and culture without spending a thing. Numerous museums and galleries, such as the National Museum of Scotland in Edinburgh, are free to enter. Also, Scotland's gorgeous landscapes are free to explore. The famous Loch Ness, for example, may be admired from many sites without having to spend money on boat cruises or other activities.

Search for bargains and discounts

When planning your trip to Scotland, be sure to check for bargains and discounts. Many attractions provide discounts for students, retirees, and families, and there are also special deals available during the off-peak season. Moreover, consider acquiring a city pass, such as the Edinburgh Pass or the Glasgow Pass, which can allow discounted entrance to famous attractions. Finally, be sure to check travel websites and apps for savings on accommodation, transport, and activities.

Discover off-the-beaten-path destinations

While Scotland's big cities and iconic attractions are surely worth visiting, there are also numerous off-the-beaten-path destinations that may provide a unique and budget-friendly experience. Scotland's countryside is full of little villages and towns that are often neglected by tourists. Visiting these regions can be a terrific opportunity to see Scotland's unique culture and scenery without spending a lot of money. Moreover, consider visiting lesser-known sights, such as tiny museums or historic sites, which can be just as fascinating as the more well-known ones.

Consider a working holiday

If you have the time and interest, a working holiday can be a wonderful opportunity to discover Scotland while also earning some money to fund your travels. Numerous farms, hostels, and other companies provide labor-for-accommodation possibilities, allowing you to stay for free in exchange for labor. Moreover, seasonal jobs, such as picking fruit or working in hospitality, can give you a consistent income while also providing you an opportunity to explore Scotland's culture and community.

Don't forget about the outdoors
One of the best things about Scotland is that many outdoor activities are free or reasonably inexpensive. Hiking, cycling, and wild swimming are all popular hobbies in Scotland as covered in the activities section, and there are many gorgeous locations to explore.

Embrace the Scottish culture
Finally, remember that Scotland's culture and history are crucial elements of the country's attractiveness, and many cultural events are free or low-cost. Joining a ceilidh, a traditional Scottish dance, or listening to live music in a local pub can be a terrific way to experience Scotland's unique culture without breaking the bank. Moreover, seeing ancient places, such as castles and ruins, can provide a fascinating peek into Scotland's history.

By timing your visit carefully, choosing budget-friendly accommodation, using public transport, planning your meals, taking advantage of free attractions, looking for deals and discounts, exploring off-the-beaten-path destinations, considering a working holiday, embracing the outdoors, and experiencing the Scottish culture, you can enjoy all that Scotland has to offer without overspending. Remember that traveling on a budget can provide unique and authentic experiences, allowing you to interact with the local culture and community in a way that a more expensive trip might not.

Getting Around

Whether you are a first-time visitor or a seasoned tourist, it's crucial to know how to get around Scotland. In this section, we will provide a thorough description of how to move around Scotland as a visitor.

By Car
Hiring a car is one of the greatest ways to discover Scotland. The country boasts a well-maintained road network that enables easy access to all major cities and communities. If you are hoping to tour the rural areas of Scotland, a car is required. Yet, driving in Scotland can be tricky, especially for first-time tourists. The roads are tiny, winding, and can be challenging to navigate. It's crucial to take your time, be patient, and pay attention to road signs and traffic lights.

By Train
Scotland has an extensive rail network that connects all major cities and communities. The trains are comfortable, swift, and economical. If you are traveling between Edinburgh and Glasgow, the train is the best alternative. The travel takes less than an hour, and trains run regularly throughout the day. If you are heading further away, the train is still an excellent alternative, but you may need to change trains at some point.

By Bus
Buses are a popular way to get across Scotland, especially if you are on a budget. The country boasts a comprehensive bus network that connects all major cities and towns. The buses are comfortable, and fares are inexpensive. If you are traveling between Edinburgh and Glasgow, the bus is a

fantastic option. The travel takes roughly an hour, and buses run frequently throughout the day. If you are traveling further away, the bus is still a decent alternative, although the journey times may be longer.

By Bicycle

If you are feeling brave, cycling is a terrific way to discover Scotland. The country features some of the most stunning cycle routes in the world, including the legendary North Coast 500. If you are planning to ride in Scotland, it's necessary to be prepared. The weather can be unpredictable, and the roads might be challenging. It's crucial to wear appropriate attire, carry lots of water and food, and be prepared for all scenarios.

By Ferry

If you are intending to explore the islands of Scotland, riding a ferry is the finest alternative. The country boasts an extensive ferry network that connects all of the major islands. The ferries are comfortable, swift, and economical. If you are planning to ride a ferry, it's crucial to reserve in advance, especially during the peak summer months.

By Air

If you are traveling great distances in Scotland, taking a flight can be ideal. The country has multiple airports that connect to major cities around the UK and Europe. The airports are well-served by airlines like British Airways, EasyJet, and Ryanair. If you are intending to travel, it's vital to book early to get the greatest discounts.

Whether you are exploring the harsh terrain of the Highlands or the dynamic cities of Glasgow and Edinburgh, there is always a way to get around. By car, train, bus, bicycle, ferry, or air, Scotland has something to offer everyone. It's crucial to plan your journey in advance, book in advance where necessary, and be prepared for all eventualities.

Shopping for Souvenirs

Renowned for its rich history, and vibrant culture, Scotland provides a wide selection of things for tourists to enjoy, including shopping for souvenirs. Scotland is a treasure trove of unique and fascinating souvenirs, and there are lots of places to find them.

One of the most popular destinations to purchase souvenirs in Scotland is Edinburgh. The city is loaded with a range of businesses that sell anything from traditional Scottish kilts and tartan scarves to handmade jewelry and Scottish whisky. The Royal Mile is the major retail strip in Edinburgh, and it is dotted with souvenir shops that offer an astounding selection of souvenirs.

If you are searching for something that is truly distinctive to Scotland, then you should consider acquiring a kilt. Kilts are an iconic aspect of Scottish culture, and they are often constructed from wool tartan. You may purchase kilts in a number of colors and patterns, and they come in a range of sizes to fit both men and women.

Another famous item that you might find in Scotland is whisky. Scotland is famed for producing some of the world's greatest whiskies, and there are several distilleries located throughout the country. You can purchase bottles of whisky from these distilleries, or you can visit one of the many whisky shops that specialize in selling unusual and unique whiskies.

If you are searching for a more traditional Scottish souvenir, then you could consider purchasing a piece of tartan. Tartan is a sort of woolen fabric that is used to manufacture kilts, scarves, and other traditional Scottish apparel items. You can find tartan in a wide range of colors and patterns, and it is commonly used to create complicated designs.

Jewelry is another favorite souvenir that you can find in Scotland. Scottish jewelry is often fashioned from silver or gold, and it commonly contains Celtic motifs. Many of the designs used in Scottish jewelry are based on old Celtic symbolism and mythology, making them both gorgeous and steeped in history.

If you are searching for something that is more whimsical, then you may try acquiring a Nessie figure. Nessie, or the Loch Ness Monster, is a legendary creature that is claimed to haunt Loch Ness in the Scottish Highlands. Nessie figurines are available in a range of forms and sizes, and they are a fun and unusual way to remember your trip to Scotland.

In addition to Edinburgh, there are many other destinations in Scotland where you can purchase souvenirs. Glasgow, for example, is another renowned shopping location that is home to a variety of shops and marketplaces. The city's Barras Market is particularly noted for its collection of unique and eccentric goods.

Buying souvenirs in Scotland is a fun and exciting experience that allows you to bring a piece of Scotland home with you. From kilts and tartan to whisky and jewelry, there is something for everyone in Scotland's souvenir shops. Thus, whether you are visiting Edinburgh, Glasgow, or any other part of Scotland, make sure to set aside some time to explore the local stores and markets and pick the perfect gift to remember your trip.

Tips for Buying

With so many distinctive and traditional Scottish things to pick from, shopping for souvenirs in Scotland can be a memorable and exciting experience. Here are some recommendations for buying souvenirs in Scotland:

Study before your trip
When you depart for Scotland, it is crucial to explore the types of mementos that are distinctive to the country. Scotland is famed for its tartan, kilts, whisky, and tweed, among other things. Understanding what to look for will make your shopping trip more fun and efficient.

Shop at traditional markets
Scotland offers several traditional markets where you may get a large selection of gifts. Some of the most popular marketplaces include the Edinburgh Farmers' Market, and the Glasgow Vintage and Flea Market. These markets provide a range of things, from artisanal meals to locally manufactured crafts and textiles.

Visit specialist shops
Specialty shops are a terrific place to find unique and high-quality goods. These shops often focus on a particular type of product, such as Scottish tartan or whisky. Visiting these businesses will provide you access to things that may not be available at typical markets or tourist shops.

Purchase from local artisans
Purchasing from local artists is a fantastic way to support the local economy and ensure that your souvenirs are real. You can find local artisans selling their creations at markets and

specialty shops throughout Scotland. Seek things that are handmade or handcrafted, as these will be more unique and likely to be of higher quality.

Search for real products

When shopping for souvenirs in Scotland, it is crucial to look for original things. Numerous souvenir shops sell mass-produced things that may not be distinctive to Scotland. Search for things that are manufactured in Scotland and that reflect the country's history and culture.

Don't be frightened to negotiate

In some marketplaces and shops, it is acceptable to haggle over the price of souvenirs. If you are buying many goods or spending a considerable amount of money, don't be hesitant to ask for a discount. Nonetheless, be professional and courteous when bargaining, and know that some sellers may not be willing to negotiate.

Consider shipping

If you are concerned about the weight and size of your keepsakes, consider sending them home. Several shops and markets offer shipping services, and this can be a convenient method to ensure that your souvenirs reach securely and without the chance of damage.

Verify customs restrictions

When you buy mementos to bring home, it is vital to examine customs laws. Certain products, such as certain types of food or alcohol, may not be authorized to be carried into your home country. Verify with your airline or customs agency to ensure that you are not infringing any rules or regulations.

By researching before your trip, visiting traditional markets and specialty shops, buying from local artisans, looking for authentic products, negotiating when appropriate, considering shipping, and checking customs regulations, you can ensure that your shopping experience is memorable and hassle-free.

Tour Package Choices

With so many things to see and do, arranging a trip to Scotland can be stressful. Yet, there are various tourist package options available that can make your vacation planning faster and more convenient.

In this part, we will explore some of the popular tourist package alternatives for Scotland.

Classic Tour Package
The Classic Tour Package is the most popular tour package in Scotland. It includes all the major tourist attractions in Scotland, including Edinburgh, Glasgow, Loch Ness, and the Highlands. The package normally lasts for 7-10 days and includes hotel, transportation, meals, and sightseeing trips. The Classic Tour Package is great for first-time tourists who wish to explore the finest of Scotland.

Adventure Tour Package
The Adventure Tour Package is designed for those who want to see the natural splendor of Scotland. This package includes activities like hiking, kayaking, and rock climbing, and covers some of the most beautiful and remote locations of Scotland, such as the Island of Skye and the Cairngorms National Park. The Adventure Tour Package is great for adventure seekers and outdoor enthusiasts.

Whiskey Tour Package
Scotland is famous for its whiskey, and the Whiskey Tour Package is created for whiskey aficionados who want to discover the distilleries of Scotland. This package includes trips to some of the most famous distilleries in Scotland, such

as Glenfiddich, Glenlivet, and Talisker. It also offers whiskey tastings and a chance to learn about the history and manufacturing of Scottish whiskey.

Golf Tour Package

Scotland is considered the home of golf, and the Golf Tour Package is created for golf aficionados who want to play some of the top golf courses in the world. This package includes accommodation at golf resorts, transportation to golf courses, and rounds of golf at some of the most prominent golf courses in Scotland, such as St. Andrews, Gleneagles, and Turnberry.

Culture Tour Package

The Cultural Tour Package is designed for those who want to explore the rich history and culture of Scotland. This trip includes tours to historical landmarks such as Edinburgh Castle, Stirling Castle, and Culloden Battlefield. It also offers cultural activities like traditional Scottish music and dance performances, and excursions to museums and galleries.

Culinary Tour Package

The Culinary Tour Package is created for foodies who wish to explore the cuisine of Scotland. This program includes tours to local markets, cookery workshops, and samples of classic Scottish dishes such as haggis, neeps, and tatties. It also includes excursions to local distilleries and breweries to try the local beer and whiskey.

Luxurious Tour Package

The Luxury Tour Package is designed for those who wish to enjoy the finest of Scotland in elegance and comfort. This package includes luxury lodging, private transportation, and exclusive activities including private tours of castles and palaces, helicopter rides over the Scottish Highlands, and private whiskey tastings.

In conclusion, Scotland has plenty to offer everyone, and there are numerous tourist package options available to appeal to diverse interests and tastes. Whether you are an adventure lover, a golf fanatic, a whiskey expert, a foodie, or a culture buff, there is a tourist package that is right for you. By choosing a tourist package, you may make your trip planning smoother, more comfortable, and more pleasurable, and experience the best of Scotland without any trouble.

Tourist Safety Tips

While Scotland is typically a safe place to visit, like any other country, travelers should take steps to protect their safety. Here are some Scotland tourist safety considerations to bear in mind while visiting:

Be mindful of your surroundings: When traveling to Scotland, it's crucial to be cautious of your surroundings. Pay attention to the people and activities around you, especially in crowded settings such as tourist sites or public transportation. Keep a watch on your valuables and avoid carrying huge quantities of cash.

Know the emergency numbers: Before your journey, make sure you know the emergency numbers in Scotland. The universal emergency number in Scotland is 999, which can be used for police, fire, or ambulance services.

Employ official transportation: If you're going to travel to Scotland, it's recommended to use official transit such as cabs or buses. Avoid using unlicensed cabs or hitchhiking, as it might be unsafe.

Dress accordingly for the weather: Scotland's weather can be unpredictable, so it's crucial to dress appropriately. Make sure you pack warm and waterproof clothing, especially if you're traveling during the winter months.

Be respectful of local customs and traditions: Scotland has a rich culture and history, and it's important to be mindful of local customs and traditions. Be conscious of any cultural or religious practices, and avoid doing anything that would upset local residents.

Avoid solitary regions at night: While Scotland is typically a safe place, it's recommended to avoid isolated areas at night. Stay in well-lit places and avoid walking alone whenever feasible.

Be cautious when using ATMs: When using ATMs in Scotland, be alert and mindful of your surroundings. Avoid utilizing ATMs that are located in secluded regions or in poorly lighted areas.

Don't drink too much alcohol: Scotland is known for its whisky and beer, but it's crucial not to drink too much alcohol. Heavy drinking might weaken your judgment and make you vulnerable to crime or accidents.

Take care when hiking or participating in outdoor activities: Scotland is known for its gorgeous natural landscapes, and hiking or participating in outdoor activities can be a terrific way to explore. Yet, it's necessary to take care to safeguard your safety. Be sure you have appropriate gear and equipment, and avoid taking needless risks.

Employ common sense: Overall, the greatest approach to keeping safe in Scotland is to apply common sense. Be alert of your surroundings, avoid unsafe circumstances, and trust your senses if something doesn't feel right.

In conclusion, Scotland is a safe place for tourists, but it's vital to take care to secure your safety. By following these Scotland tourist safety recommendations, you can have a safe and pleasurable journey to this beautiful country.

Festival and Events

One of the best ways to explore Scottish culture is through its festivals and events. Scotland has a diverse selection of festivals and events throughout the year, which highlight everything from traditional music and dance to contemporary art and culture. In this part, we will explore some of the most popular festivals and events in Scotland.

Edinburgh Festival Fringe

The Edinburgh Festival Fringe is the world's largest arts festival, bringing thousands of tourists from all over the world. The festival takes place in August and features a varied spectrum of performances, including theater, comedy, music, and dance. The Fringe is an open-access event, meaning that anyone can perform, which has led to the discovery of many new artists.

Royal Edinburgh Military Tattoo

The Royal Edinburgh Military Tattoo is a stunning event that takes place every August. The event comprises performances by military bands from all around the world, as well as exhibits of traditional Scottish music and dancing. The highlight of the Tattoo is the massed pipes and drums, where hundreds of pipers and drummers perform together in perfect synchronization.

Celtic Connections

Celtic Connections is a music festival that takes place in January in Glasgow. The event honors traditional Scottish music as well as music from throughout the world. The festival comprises a range of concerts, seminars, and discussions, and attracts guests from all around the world.

Hogmanay

Hogmanay is Scotland's famed New Year's Eve event. The festival takes place in Edinburgh and incorporates a number of traditional Scottish festivities, including a torchlight procession, a ceilidh, and a firework show. The Hogmanay events are known for their festive atmosphere and are a must-see for anybody visiting Scotland over the New Year holiday.

Burns Night

Burns Night is a commemoration of the life and work of the legendary Scottish poet Robert Burns. The celebration takes place annually on January 25th and incorporates traditional Scottish food, drink, and music. The centerpiece of the event is the performance of Burns' poems, especially his famous Address to a Haggis.

The Royal Highland Show

The Royal Highland Show is Scotland's largest agricultural event and takes place in June. The event incorporates a number of activities, including animal shows, food and drink demonstrations, and traditional Scottish music and dancing. The Royal Highland Fair is a terrific way to see Scottish rural life and is a must-see for anyone interested in farming or agriculture.

The Shetland Folk Festival

The Shetland Folk Festival is a celebration of traditional music that takes place in May in the Shetland Islands. The festival comprises concerts by musicians from throughout the world, as well as workshops and seminars. The event is a terrific way to discover the distinct culture and traditions of the Shetland Islands.

In conclusion, Scotland offers a broad choice of festivals and events throughout the year, celebrating everything from traditional music and dance to contemporary art and culture. Whether you are interested in traditional Scottish activities or more contemporary events, there is something for everyone in Scotland's festival calendar. The festivals and events in Scotland give a unique opportunity to explore Scottish culture and traditions and are a must-see for anybody visiting the nation.

Milton Keynes UK
Ingram Content Group UK Ltd.
UKHW021356130824
1249UKWH00066B/1573